This Notebook Belongs To

____

Made in the USA
Las Vegas, NV
25 February 2023

68147868R00073